God Made Me

Helen Haidle
Illustrated by Rick Incrocci

The text of this book may be sung to the tune of
"Twinkle, Twinkle, Little Star."

CPH
Concordia Publishing House

Thank You, God, for my two eyes.
I see birds fly in the skies.
Watch my kite sail way up high,
While the puffy clouds float by.

When it's dark, I squint my eyes,

Counting stars and fireflies.

Thank You, God, for my two ears.
Soft and noisy sounds I hear.
Booming drums so **LOUD** and clear.
Horns and whistles far and near.

Listen closely—can you hear
Mommy whispering in my ear?

Thank You, God, for my two hands.
I like digging in the sand.
Building castles on the land;
When the waves come, will they stand?

Poking, patting with my hands,
Making sandy wonderlands.

Thank You, God, for feet to run,

Chasing after everyone.

Dancing barefoot in the sun;
Tapping to the fiddle strum.

Jumping, climbing—oh, what *FUN*!
Running 'til the day is done!

Thank You, God, for toes that tap
To the music—*tap, tap, tap.*

Thanks for fingers I can snap,
Making rhythm—*snap, snap, snap.*

Thank You, God, for hands that clap;

When I'm happy—*clap, clap, clap!*

Thank You, God, for legs so strong.
They are growing tall and long.

Thank You, God, for arms You gave.
Arms that carry, reach, and wave.

Thank You, God, for lots of hair!

Straight or curly, dark or fair.

It is fun to use my nose—

Smell baked bread! Come, smell the rose!

Thank You, God, for teeth that chew
Apples, corn, and carrots too.

My mouth opens big and wide,
So my lunch can fit inside.

I am thankful for my tongue.
Tasting food is lots of fun.

Salt and pepper, candy sweets;
Sour pickles, ice-cream treats.

Grandma's apple pie tastes good.

Thank You, God, for tasty food!

Voices help you make a noise;
Talk to other girls and boys.

I learned how to talk and speak.
I can holler, shout, and squeak.

God gave me a voice to sing.
Thank You, God, for **EVERYTHING!**